Holding On
and
Letting Go

Finding Hope In
the Midst of Chaos

Tom Lemler

Holding On and Letting Go:
Finding Hope In the Midst of Chaos

Copyright ©2018
ISBN-13: 978-1-946319-04-3
ISBN-10: 1-946319-04-X

For information:

Tom Lemler
Impact Prayer Ministry
2730 S Ironwood Dr
South Bend IN 46614
www.impactprayerministry.com
tlemler@gapministry.com

Loss affects us all very deeply and very uniquely. It is in the times of greatest chaos that we need gentle reminders about the things we must hold on to which will bring us hope, and about the things we must let go of so that healing may begin. This devotional hopes to tackle a few of those "hold on to" and "let go of" choices each of us are faced with in the midst of chaos.

This book is dedicated in grateful acknowledgment to God who has always found ways to give me hope in the midst of the chaos I often find myself in. I thank IDES for helping to plant in my mind the idea for this book and for their unwavering commitment to carry the hope of Jesus into the heart of disaster relief. And I thank the Deer Run congregation and my family — each of them helps me in a great way to understand the need to hold on to some things while letting go of others as they support the calling and gifting God has put in my life. To all of these, and to you my readers, thank you!

Table of Contents

Introduction

Disaster. No matter what form that it arrives in, it seems to always have the ability to shake us to our very core. There is rarely enough warning, if any, and even with warning our preparations generally don't really get us ready for the emotional turmoil that ensues — let alone the physical losses.

This book was written to help you spend time with God as you wrestle through the issues of the chaos you now face. Whether used alone with God or in a group setting with others that are recovering from disaster, connecting with God through the process of holding on and letting go really is the key element in finding hope in the midst of any chaos of life.

As you go through the book, each chapter will alternate between focusing on something you should hold on to and something you will find yourself needing to let go of. Each chapter begins with a statement of focus and a scripture to get you started in God's Word. If you can, look up the scripture reference in its context and meditate on God's Word about holding on, or letting go, of the topic being discussed.

6

Following the topic and scripture page will come some devotional writing which flows from my prayer time focused on the subject at hand. It will include questions to help you think more clearly about how holding on or letting go will help bring hope. There will be direction and suggestions on how to focus your prayer time as you seek to grow in relationship with God through the pain of disaster. As you go through the devotional writing, spend time with God in prayer for yourself and for the people around you to have a greater grasp of living with the hope offered by Christ

Each chapter will include some space for you to record your interaction with God. Jot down your thoughts, your prayers, other scriptures that God brings to mind during your time with Him, and/or changes in your attitude or actions that He reveals you need to make. Use this journal section to help you remember and to help you grow.

In prayer,
Tom Lemler
Impact Prayer Ministry

Hold On

To

One Another

*"And our hope for you is firm,
because we know that just as you
share in our sufferings, so also you
share in our comfort."*
(2 Corinthians 1:7)

Hold On To One Another

How alone does your current situation make you feel? Why? Are there others affected by the same thing you are currently going through? Do you think they feel alone? Why? Are there people in similar circumstances who would benefit from your willingness to hold on to them? Do you know people who have already been through what you are dealing with that you could hold on to? Who?

In the midst of loss, it is God's desire to bring seeds of comfort to you through people who have received the same comfort that you now need. No matter the loss, it will generally feel amplified if you must face it alone. Sometimes the loss is very personal and the enemy would want you to think no one will understand. Other times the loss is one suffered by many others and the enemy will try to convince you that people have enough grief of their own to worry about. Neither of those could be further from the truth. Whether in our most private pain or a very public loss, God has helped to carry others through the very nature of what you are dealing with. While it may be fun to "rejoice with those who rejoice", it is just as necessary to "weep with those who weep". Holding on to one another won't solve all the problems, or bring back what was lost, but when those we hold on to are holding on to God, we discover we truly are not alone.

As you pray today, ask God to help you find those who will be someone you can hold on to. Pray that God would give you the strength needed so that you can be someone others will hold on to, even in your weakness. Pray that you would find, and be, a community that holds on to one another.

_____

_____

_____

_____

_____

_____

_____

_____

_____

_____

_____

Let Go
Of Things
You Can't
Control

"Who of you by worrying can add a single hour to his life ?"
(Matthew 6:27)

Let Go Of Things You Can't Control

What part of your current situation feels most beyond your control? How much do you worry about things you can't change? Are there things in the midst of your current chaos that you do have some control over? How much does the lack of control over some things keep you from taking control of what you can?

Facing a disaster of any kind often brings with it a bewildering feeling of having no control over anything that is going on. The truth is, even in our most controlling moments, we have far less control than we would like to admit. When faced with loss, it is important to identify specific things that we simply can't control. Some of those things may well be the disaster which brought about the loss, as well as the timetable for any recovery. Letting go of control doesn't mean that we give up, or that we don't put any effort into doing what we can, rather it means that we learn to accept that our recovery will take place on a timetable that will likely change often and is very different than what we would want. Letting go of the things we can't control can

12

be one of the early steps toward trusting God to bring hope in the midst of our chaos. It is important to remember that just because we can't control what is going on, it doesn't mean that it is out of His control. Often times identifying what we can't control, and then letting go of it, frees us to take appropriate action in the areas that can make a difference in our recovery. Letting go of what we can't control helps to bring hope not only because it shows our trust of God, but it allows us concentrate on the things we can still do.

As you pray, ask God to help you let go of the things that you can't control. Pray that He would give you wisdom in distinguishing between that which is simply difficult and that which isn't yours to take care of. Pray that your trust of Him would grow as you learn to let go of control.

_____

_____

_____

_____

_____

_____

_____

_____

_____

Hold On To What You Have

"I am coming soon. Hold on to what you have, so that no one will take your crown."
(Revelation 3:11)

Hold On To What You Have

What do you have? How difficult is it to answer that question? Why? In your current situation, do you tend to think more about what you have lost or about what you still have? Why? Even if it seems you have lost everything, how focused are you at holding on to faith?

One of the most difficult things for many people to do in the midst of loss is to see what they haven't lost. Our mind gets so focused on the disaster we faced that we become blinded to the things we still have. As we discussed earlier, one of those things should be the people God will bring into our life to provide help and comfort. The old hymn that says, "Count your blessings, name them one by one", may sound trite when recovering from a disaster, but taking inventory of what you do have really is a good practice at any time. When we begin to count more than possessions, we often find much that is within our grasp to hold on to that should give us at least glimmers of hope. For most of us, there seems to be something within our nature that longs to possess things that we can call our

15

own. Even the most open and sharing child seems to learn how to say "Mine!" all on their own. So as you do inventory of both the tangible and intangible things that you still have, find hope as you hold on to the things you have and especially to the things that can never be taken from you.

As you pray, ask God to help you grieve what you have lost even as you identify what you still have. Pray that you would find hope and comfort through holding on to relationships that continue in the midst of your chaos. Pray that your time of inventory would help you discover important things that God would have you hold on to. Pray for the courage to hold loosely even as you hold on to what you have.

_____

_____

_____

_____

_____

_____

_____

_____

_____

Day Four

Let Go
Of Anger

"'In your anger do not sin': Do not let the sun go down while you are still angry, and do not give the devil a foothold."
(Ephesians 4:26-27)

Let Go Of Anger

Does the current chaos you are experiencing make you angry? Should it? How does anger influence the way you respond to both people and your situation? Does anger typically cause a good or bad response? Explain. How will letting go of anger free you to see your situation more clearly?

Anger is a natural emotion and reaction, especially when faced with unexpected and unreasonable loss. The problem with anger in the midst of chaos is that it tends to cloud the vision of both our mind and our eyes. When the Bible says, "in your anger do not sin", I believe the instruction is to acknowledge our anger and deal with it so that we can let it go before it infects our actions. While there may be things, circumstances, and even people that you feel you have a right to be angry with, feeding the anger will only make it grow to the point that it adds to the problem. Letting go of the anger allows us to address the chaos, and even address the cause of the chaos, from a healthy position of resolution rather than hatred. When we learn to be angry at the right things, we find that we can allow God to use our anger as an internal motivation for us to make changes we need to make. It is then that we are able to let go of that anger so that we can begin to see hope in the midst of our chaos. Unresolved and/or unaddressed anger destroys hope and it is in the addressing and resolving of our anger that we find we can let the anger go and allow hope to grow.

As you pray, ask God to help you understand why you feel angry, and specifically who or what you feel angry toward. Pray that you would not simply attempt to hide the anger, but address it in ways that allow you to let go of it. Pray that you would know the hope that comes through letting go of anger after it has been dealt with.

_____

_____

_____

_____

_____

_____

_____

_____

_____

_____

Hold On

To

What Is Good

"Test everything. Hold on to the good."

(1 Thessalonians 5:21)

Hold On To What Is Good

What do you see right now that is good in your life? In the fog of chaos, how hard do you have to look in order to find something good? Why? How does finding the good that God wants you to cling to help you endure your current situation?   What good do you need to hold on to today in order to have hope for tomorrow?

Holding on to what is good can be extremely difficult when the chaos you are in creates such a darkness that seeing any good is nearly impossible. Yet often times, it is in those very dark hours that even a small glimmer of goodness shines most brightly. I'm not talking about some sort of Pollyanna "it's all good" kind of mentality, but rather a trust in a God who is good. While there may be moments and days when it doesn't feel like it, God is good and loves His children with an unchanging love.   While it's not necessarily true that "every cloud has a silver lining", we know that good often has to be looked for in order to be found. As you walk through the fog of disaster, take the time to look for good. Look for it in the surroundings you face every day. Look for it in the people that gather to

21

help. Look for it in those who God will bring alongside you to provide hope. Look for it in yourself. And most importantly, look for it in God. When your world looks darkest, don't let the darkness hide all the good that remains. When you look for and hold on to the good that God desires for you, He will grow within you a hope in the midst of your current chaos.

As you pray, ask God to help you see beyond the difficulty you to find the good that remains. Pray that you would hold on to the good that you find in life and in people. Pray for the courage to be the good that others can hold on to in their need. Pray that you would find hope as you hold on to God's goodness revealed in a variety of ways.

_____

_____

_____

_____

_____

_____

_____

_____

_____

Let Go

Of Worry

"Therefore do not worry about tomorrow, for tomorrow will worry about itself. Each day has enough trouble of its own."
(Matthew 6:34)

Let Go Of Worry

What worries you the most about your current situation? How would you rate your current level of worry? Why? Does your worry focus on what has happened, what might happen, or on what you can do today? What is the difference? How will letting go of worry help you to have hope in the midst of your situation of chaos?

Worry carried to an extreme can result in a paralysis that makes it impossible to see and move beyond your current circumstances. When surrounded by the unknown of chaos, worry can easily take root in the heart of even the most carefree person. When disaster forces us to let go of many things we would have rather kept, worrying about what we have left or how we will ever recover seems almost natural and even helpful in some way. Yet when we give worry a foothold it isn't long before it takes over and keeps us from seeing the daily steps of recovery that are in front of us. Worrying about yesterday is a form of second-guessing that does us no good as no amount of worry will let us go back and change what has already happened. Worrying about tomorrow is just as fruitless because we can't predict the future, let alone control it. Today's worry might have limited usefulness, but only if it motivates us to take the action steps necessary to bring about the change we need. But even today's worry must be let go of as we trust God to bring hope into our current situation of chaos.

As you pray, ask God to give you a peace that dispels harmful worry as you trust in Him. Pray that your concern for today would drive you to a responsiveness to God rather than to a mindset of worry. Pray that you would know the great hope that God wants to give you as you let go of worry.

_____

_____

_____

_____

_____

_____

_____

_____

_____

_____

Hold On

To

Instruction

"Hold on to instruction, do not let it
go; guard it well, for it is your life."
(Proverbs 4:13)

.

Hold On To Instruction

Are you teachable? How do you know? What is the difference between being told what to do and being given instruction? Which do you prefer? Why? How difficult is it for you to follow instructions that you don't like? Do you do it anyway? What are some instructions, from God and from others, that you need to hold on to right now that would give you hope in the midst of your chaos?

You've probably heard the phrase countless times — "When all else fails, read the instructions." Well, when disaster strikes we would do well to consider that all else has failed and it is time to hold on to instruction. This instruction will take many forms. The most important in the long-term will be to continue to hold on to instruction from God's Word. Yet, even as we do that, there will be instruction that people will offer that can lead us through the chaos and toward a road of recovery. Caution must be used when we hold on to instruction as not everyone giving instruction will always be doing so with pure and helpful motives. Nonetheless, through time spent with God, we must seek out wise instruction and hold on to it even as we put it into practice. You see, practice really is the key to making good use of instruction. Whether it is the instruction of God's Word or the instruction from someone who has experienced a disaster similar to what you are going through, it does little good to simply accumulate instruction if we're not willing to use it. When you hold on to godly instruction, you will find He sets you on a path of hope in the midst of your chaos.

As you pray, ask God for wisdom to discern between instruction which is good and that which is not. Pray that you would be active in holding on to instruction as you put it into practice. Pray for courage to share the instructions you are holding on to when it will help others.

_____

_____

_____

_____

_____

_____

_____

_____

_____

Let Go

Of

Selfishness

"Do nothing out of selfish ambition or vain conceit, but in humility consider others better than yourselves."
(Philippianas 2:3)

Let Go Of Selfishness

How easy is it for you to share? Does that answer change based on how much of something you feel you have? Why? When help arrives in the midst of chaos, would you rather see someone else helped first or yourself? Why? If you find something being offered for free, do you take as much as you can or only what you need? How can looking out for the interests of others help you have hope when in the midst of chaos?

When you lose much, it can be natural to cling to whatever you can manage to obtain. Selfishness is one of those traits that is often easier to see in others than to see in ourselves. Many times when a group experiences a disaster together, a comradery is developed that makes people open to sharing anything and everything that can be salvaged. Other times, however, loss can lead us to selfishly cling to things we don't even have a use for just because we don't want to let go. Overcoming chaos means we let go of selfishness and learn that others have needs to be met as well. Every line has a beginning and an end and while we would probably all prefer to be at the beginning, that is simply not possible. Letting go of selfishness doesn't mean we no longer care, but rather now we care about everyone being taken care of and not just our self. Especially in disaster when relief supplies are often limited, it is important that we let go of selfishness as we gain a shared concern for everyone who is also suffering. When we don't know if additional help is coming, it can be very tempting to take all we can whether we need it right now or not. Letting go of selfishness helps us have hope in the midst of our chaos as we find joy in sharing with others.

As you pray, ask God to help you see any ways of selfishness that may exist in you. Pray that you would continue to share freely, even in chaotic situations, as you learn to let go of all traces of selfishness.

_____

_____

_____

_____

_____

_____

_____

Hold On

To

Courage

"But Christ is faithful as a son over God's house. And we are his house, if we hold on to our courage and the hope of which we boast."
(Hebrews 3:6)

Hold On To Courage

What is the greatest difficulty that you have overcome in the past? What gave you the courage to keep going when things seemed out of control? How much courage will it take to overcome your current situation? How can an awareness of God's faithfulness help you hold on to the courage you need now?

When fear tells us to quit, courage drives us to keep going. Very few times in life are the obstacles we must face more obvious than in the midst of disaster. Often times the difference between succumbing to disaster and overcoming it comes down to having the courage to keep on going, and keep on trusting God, no matter what. For most of us, we don't think a lot about courage, or fear, until something happens that puts our courage to the test. In those times when we find many reasons to fear, we are left with a choice — give in to doubt or hold on to courage. When surrounded by chaos, courage is what allows us to keep moving forward even in the face of our fears. It can be difficult to look ahead when the present situation seems so dark and overwhelming, but courage will help us see beyond the darkness and into the light that is God's presence. As you consider your future, it is important that you keep your gaze lifted beyond the current chaos even as you deal with it on a daily basis. Knowing that you belong to an eternal family should give you a greater perspective in how to face each day's struggles with courage. With Jesus as our example and strength, we hold on to courage in the midst of chaos and find that our fears no longer have control.

As you pray, ask God to help you understand the things in your current situation that cause you to be filled with fear. Pray that you would live with courage from God that helps you to face each day's fears and keep going. Pray that you would draw courage from being a part of God's eternal family.

_____

_____

_____

_____

_____

_____

_____

Let Go

Of

Guilt

"Let us draw near to God with a sincere heart in full assurance of faith, having our hearts sprinkled to cleanse us from a guilty conscience and having our bodies washed with pure water."
(Hebrews 10:22)

Let Go Of Guilt

How often do you think about the cause of your current chaos? Why? Do you feel you need someone to blame when things go wrong? What happens when the disaster you face isn't really caused by a person? How often do you look back in an attempt to see if you could have done anything differently to avoid or lessen the chaos you are in? How will letting go of guilt in the midst of your chaos give you greater freedom to see beyond the immediate?

Second-guessing is a game that has no winners. All of us can look back and see things we could have, and even should have, done differently. Even if we are at fault in some way, holding on to guilt is a dangerous thing that does no good for anyone. One of my favorite verses says, "If we confess our sins, He is faithful and just to forgive us our sins and cleanse us from all unrighteousness." When we choose God's forgiveness, we can let go of the guilt that the enemy wants to haunt us with. Sometimes the guilt we hold on to isn't even reasonable, but when there is no one else to blame, we blame our self. Letting go of guilt doesn't mean that we

36

ignore anything we may have done, but rather it means we deal with it and move on. It often feels like the enemy does everything he can to fill us with shame so that we hold on to our guilt. If there is anything to be ashamed of, we must take care of it appropriately and then fully release it to God. When we let go of guilt we find that we not only live with greater peace, but we are also better equipped to handle whatever the day brings.

As you pray, ask God to help you identify any guilty feelings that you may have. Pray that you would see clearly what was your responsibility and what wasn't so that anything that may need taken care of can be dealt with. Pray that you would know the sweet peace that comes from God's grace as you let go of guilt.

_____

_____

_____

_____

_____

_____

_____

_____

Hold On

To

Righteousness

"I will maintain my righteousness and never let go of it; my conscience will not reproach me as long as I live."
(Job 27:6)

Hold On To Righteousness

Have you ever had someone ask you to do something that you knew wasn't right? How did you respond? Does your response differ based on how doing so would benefit you? Why? How important is righteousness to you? Why? How important is righteousness to God? How will holding on to righteousness in the midst of your chaos give you hope as you look toward the future?

Disaster and chaos can bring out the best in people and it can bring out the worst. There will always be those who try to take advantage of the hurting and there will often be temptations to take "shortcuts" to recovery. God's desire is that we would hold on to righteousness for His Name's sake. How we deal with the disasters we face, and how we deal with people during those disasters, will say much to a watching world about the God we claim to serve. When we hold on to righteousness, we do everything above board and we treat all people openly and fairly. When I think of disaster and chaos in the Bible there are many examples, but perhaps none as extreme as the story of Job. Even while lacking the "backstory" that we have regarding the source of the disasters he faced, Job knew that holding on to the righteousness of God was his only hope for the future. When we hold on to a righteousness that is ours through Jesus Christ, we find that our current disaster doesn't have to define us or define how we treat others. It is in the righteousness of Christ that we have hope that extends beyond any chaos that we are experiencing today.

As you pray, ask God to help you to always see and do the things which are right. Pray that your mind would not be clouded by the fog of chaos as you make decisions each day. Pray that you would not only know the right things to do, but that you would do them. Pray that the eternal reward of holding on to righteousness would fill you with hope today.

_____

_____

_____

_____

_____

_____

_____

_____

Let Go Of Fear

"There is no fear in love. But perfect love drives out fear, because fear has to do with punishment. The one who fears is not made perfect in love."
(1 John 4:18)

Let Go Of Fear

What has been the most frightening part of the current chaos you are in? Why? Are there things that can be done to take care of the cause of the fear? What? How does fear influence your recovery efforts? Is letting go of fear the same as eliminating it? Explain. What would it take for you to let go of fear today so that you can live with hope in the midst of your chaos?

Many times when something bad happens in our life we find our self just waiting for the other shoe to drop. Our response to disaster and chaos is often a fear that something else, something much worse, is just around the corner. While there may or may not be something worse coming, we must learn to let go of fear in order to accurately handle the current chaos we are dealing with. In many ways, fear and worry are twins which try to rob us of the value of today by making our thoughts dwell on the "what ifs" of tomorrow. While there is a healthy fear which keeps us from doing things that would harm us, it is the unhealthy, paralyzing fear that we must let go of in order to find hope in the midst of our chaos. We must face each moment, and

42

whatever it brings, with an absence of the fear that wants to make us stop moving forward. The only real way to let go of fear is to turn to God in a greater trust for each moment. And yes, that sounds a lot simpler than it is. Replacing fear with trust is a difficult process that can only be done one step at a time. When you do learn to take those steps, you will find that letting go of fear opens up a window of hope in the midst of whatever chaos you face.

As you pray, ask God to help you identify the different fears you have in the midst of your current situation. Pray that you would have wisdom to know which fears are helping to protect you and which fears are holding you back from what you need to do. Pray for that you would learn to trust God enough to let go of your fears that are stealing your hope.

_____

_____

_____

_____

_____

_____

_____

Hold On

To

Sound Teaching

*"So then, brothers, stand firm and
hold to the teachings we passed on
to you, whether by word of mouth or
by letter."*
(2 Thessalonians 2:15)

Hold On To Sound Teaching

What is the best advice you have ever received? Do you still follow it? Why? Have you ever been taught something that you later found out was not true? How did you feel? How does the teaching that you hold on to influence the actions you take when times are chaotic? What is some sound teaching that you need to hold on to and put into practice today?

If something sounds too good to be true, it probably is. Unfortunately, in the midst of chaos we often grasp at anything that offers a semblance of stability. It is in times of disaster that it becomes extra critical that we seek out sound advice and teaching. When we are in desperate need of help, it becomes very difficult to see through the motives of offers that are actually designed to take from us rather than help us. It is especially true in these times that we must recall the sound teachings that we have learned in times past. While good advice from friends and family can be quite helpful, there is nothing as lasting as holding on to the sound instruction of God's Word. Part of the beauty of God's Word is that it portrays people that sound eerily

45

similar to you and I. Through their stories and examples, we find the value of holding on to God's teachings in the midst of disaster — and we find the consequences of not doing so. While there will be many decisions you must make that will feel rushed, none will be so hurried that you can't take time to ask God for His instruction. Holding on to sound teaching will give us a strong foothold to stand against not only the schemes of satan, but also against the schemes of those who would want to take advantage of our misfortune.

As you pray, ask God to refresh your mind with the sound teaching you have learned from Him — and of Him. Pray that you would see through all the bad advice and hold on to sound teaching as you find hope in the midst of your chaos.

_____

_____

_____

_____

_____

_____

_____

_____

_____

Let Go Of Greed

"Then he said to them, 'Watch out!
Be on your guard against all kinds of
greed; a man's life does not consist
in the abundance of his
possessions.'"
(Luke 12:15)

Let Go Of Greed

How much is enough? Are you sure? What determines that answer in your life? Why? Is greed more about what you have or about what you want? Why? Have you ever missed out on something you wanted, or needed, because of the greed of someone else? How did you feel? How will letting go of greed help you to not only have hope, but help you to share hope with others?

"I've lost so much, it is only fair that I take whatever I can get." Perhaps you've heard someone say that, or even said it yourself. Such an attitude may not be greedy in and of itself, but it definitely has the seeds of greed when the "whatever" is limited. Particularly when recovery resources are limited, it can be very difficult to consider the needs of anyone but ourselves. In fact, the fog of chaos can make it appear in our mind as if we're the only one who is in real need. For most of us, the seeds of greed are hidden well enough that we rarely recognize them. In fact, even considering that we need to let go of greed probably seems a bit abrasive to many of us. Yet without a deliberate effort to let it go, greed has a way of weaving itself into our mind in ways that eventually come out. Like so many other things that we need to let go of, doing so will require that we replace it with something so that the hole left is filled. When it comes to letting go of greed, it is the act of sharing that best fills the hole left by greed's absence. Letting go of greed allows us to see the needs of our friends, families, and neighbors to be as equally important as our own — or maybe even more so. Letting go of greed gives us hope as we not only look to God to provide all our needs, but we also trust Him to do so.

As you pray, ask God to help you examine your heart and mind for any seeds of greed that you need to let go of. Pray that you would look to the needs of others even above your own. Pray that you would know the hope God desires to give as you let go of greed and learn to share.

_____

_____

_____

_____

_____

_____

Hold On

To

The Goal

"Not that I have already obtained all this, or have already been made perfect, but I press on to take hold of that for which Christ Jesus took hold of me."
(Philippians 3:12)

Hold On To the Goal

What are your goals in life? What is your primary goal? What are you doing to reach your goals? Have you ever had a goal that was important to you at one time but you have quit pursuing? Why? As you look at your current situation, what is your goal for today? Why? What goal do you need to hold on to in order for you to have hope in the midst of your current chaos?

Life is full of distractions for everyone, but for those in the midst of the chaos of disaster, the temptation to lose sight of life's goals becomes even greater. In fact, sometimes it is critical that we develop daily goals that are manageable, even while we keep an eye on the eternal goal that ought to guide our life. If our ultimate goal is to take hold of the eternal life to which God has called us, then perhaps we ought to consider what the pursuit of that looks like each day in the midst of our disaster and recovery. Cutting through the fog of chaos often requires a flexibility that makes it easy to lose sight of not only the eternal goal, but the short term goals that get us beyond the disaster and into recovery. When our plans are changed by situations and circumstances beyond our control, it can be easy to question whether any of our goals are even attainable. The answer to that question will have a lot to do with the source of those goals. Disaster has a way of refining our goals like little else can. When so much is lost, it can be difficult to have a goal beyond just getting through another day. Yet when we hold on not only to the goal of getting through the day but also to the eternal goal we most long for, we find the hope needed to keep going.

As you pray, ask God to help you examine the goals you think most important. Pray that you would evaluate all of your goals in light of the eternal goal that God has taken hold of you for. Pray that you would hold on to the goals that God has for you even as you endure the chaos of life.

_____

_____

_____

_____

_____

_____

_____

_____

Let Go
Of
Doubt

"But when he asks, he must believe and not doubt, because he who doubts is like a wave of the sea, blown and tossed by the wind."
(James 1:6)

Let Go Of Doubt

How confident do you tend to be? What is this confidence level based on? What types of things are most likely to destroy your confidence? Do you have doubt? Has your current situation increased your doubts? Why? Do the doubts related to the uncertainty you face make you question if recovery is even possible? What would it take for you to let go of doubt so that you can find hope?

For many, disaster can fill us with doubt so quickly that we lose hope that anything will ever be okay again. While uncertainty in life is a given, serious doubt has a way of growing and infecting us way beyond that which is unknown. When we allow our doubts to grow, we find that we begin to doubt if anyone even cares and those thoughts will eventually lead us to doubt God's love. When doubt fills our mind, it isn't long before every thought we have is filtered through that doubt. Letting go of doubt doesn't remove all uncertainty, but it can open our minds to being able to trust both people and God more fully. When doubt no longer has control of our thoughts, we are set free to walk by faith

54

as we trust in God. We may not know where the immediate help that we need will come from, but we trust that God will be with us both now and forevermore. Letting go of doubt doesn't mean that we all of a sudden get all of the answers we are looking for, but it means we no longer allow the lack of answers to have control over us. Letting go of doubt allows us to be filled with a faith that trusts God to provide whatever we ask according to His will.

As you pray, ask God to help you evaluate how much the uncertainties of life have grown into doubt in your mind. Pray that you would learn to face the unknown with faith rather than doubt. Pray that God would help you seek His will as you walk, and ask, by faith each day. Pray that you would have greater hope in the midst of chaos as you let go of doubt.

_____

_____

_____

_____

_____

_____

_____

Hold On

To

Memories

"And I will make every effort to see that after my departure you will always be able to remember these things."
(2 Peter 1:15)

Hold On To Memories

What is the earliest memory that you have? Is it a good memory? How important are memories to you? Why? Are there things people tell you about that you wish you could remember? Why? What are some things that help you hold on to the important things you ought to remember? How will holding on to memories help you have hope in the midst of your current chaos?

There are some losses that simply can't be fixed or restored to the way things were before. Whether we sit in the rubble of a destroyed home or at the graveside of a child, the realization often hits that nothing will ever be the same. Holding on to memories in the midst of chaos can be a good thing — if you have good memories to hold on to. If not, perhaps it is time to make some good memories that will help carry you through the chaos you are experiencing. Throughout scripture, it is apparent that God is very aware of the forgetfulness of mankind. He is also aware of how important it is to remember the things He has done, so He often gave instructions to His people to set up feasts, monuments, meals, and other means to serve as reminders not just of what He has done, but also reminders to share with others what He has done. Our memories are what carries us through the hours of darkness as we await restoration — whether the temporary restoration from our current disaster or the permanent restoration in eternity. As we hold on to the memories of God's work not only throughout history, but His work specifically in our life, we are reminded of His faithfulness that can carry us through our chaos.

As you pray, ask God to help you recall the memories of His working in your life. Pray that you would not just hold on to the memories, but that you would share them with others. Pray that you would find comfort in the memories you have — even memories of things that have been lost. Pray that you would hold on to memories in a way that brings hope for the future.

_____

_____

_____

_____

_____

_____

_____

Let Go

Of

Pride

"Pride only breeds quarrels, but wisdom is found in those who take advice."
(Proverbs 13:10)

Let Go Of Pride

Are you a prideful person? Is pride always bad? Explain. Do you like asking for help? Why? Do you ever give up on something when you know it could be done if you had a little help? Why? Are there things you expect others to do that you won't? Why? How will letting go of pride help both you and others as you live in the midst of chaos?

For many, one of the hardest things to do is to ask for help because it requires us to admit we can't do something on our own. Pride wants to isolate us from those that God may well have surrounded us with for the very purpose of providing the help we desperately need. Letting go of pride will help us not only admit our need, but it open us up to allowing others to help us in ways that perhaps only they can. In the fog of disaster, pride can also creep in and say, "I didn't deserve this." While true or not, the problem with such a statement is that it focuses on self rather than on the shared loss by all that experience the same, or similar, disaster. When our focus is on what we did or didn't deserve, we will rarely lift our eyes far enough to see the shared suffering that is experienced by many around us. Pride is a tool of isolation as it attempts to lift us up above everyone else. When we let go of pride, we can not only see those around us who are also struggling, we can often see ways that we can help them even as we ourselves are being helped. It is when we replace pride with humility that we find ourselves lifted up by God in order to be His shining light in the midst of chaos. Letting go of pride brings hope as it helps us love people as Jesus does.

As you pray, ask God to help you examine yourself for any traces of pride that lifts yourself above someone else. Pray that God would help you remove all elements of pride that keep you from asking for and receiving the help you need. Pray that you would let go of pride as you learn and practice humility while seeking to live like Jesus.

_____

_____

_____

_____

_____

_____

_____

_____

Hold On

To

God

*"For I am the LORD, your God,
who takes hold of your right hand
and says to you, Do not fear;
I will help you."*
(Isaiah 41:13)

Hold On To God

Have you ever felt abandoned by people? Are there people who likely feel that you have abandoned them? Have you ever felt abandoned by God? Why? What do you do when you feel alone? How difficult is it to hold on to God when you find yourself in the midst of chaos? Why? What comfort does God give you when you do hold on to Him in the midst of disaster?

Recovery is rarely as fast as we would like and often never as complete as we would hope. It is in the process of overcoming that we must hold on to God every step of the way. God has promised that He will never leave us nor forsake us, but I know a lot of people who live life distant from God — many as a reaction to some disaster in their life. The problem isn't that God left, but rather that the enemy convinces us that God doesn't care so we might as well let go. Holding on to God is a matter of faith and sometimes we just need to join the person in scripture in saying, "Lord, I believe. Help my unbelief!" Even when it is unclear if and when life will ever be "normal" again, holding on to God will give us a sure foundation for whatever the days ahead will

63

bring. Yes, there will likely be people that abandon us and even people that we abandon, but we must be careful to not let our failures define God. As we hold on to God we find that He also has a firm hold on us with a desire to see us through the troubles of life. When we hold on to God in the midst of our chaos, we find that we not only have a point of stability in our life but that He will use us to help others see Him as the reason for our hope.

As you pray, thank God for always being there for you to hold on to. Pray that you would not allow the actions or inactions of people to entice you into letting go of God. Pray that you would hold on to God in such a way that He provides hope to you and to those around you.

_____

_____

_____

_____

_____

_____

_____

_____

_____

27159356R00039

Made in the USA
Columbia, SC
23 September 2018